Copyright © 2024 Chimezie Igwe

All rights reserved

The characters and events portrayed in this book are fictitious. Any similarity to real persons, living or dead, is coincidental and not intended by the author.

No part of this book may be reproduced, or stored in a retrieval system, or transmitted in any form or by any means, electronic, mechanical, photocopying, recording, or otherwise, without express written permission of the publisher.

ISBN: 9798321089743
Imprint: Independently published

Cover design by: Art Painter
Library of Congress Control Number: 2018675309
Printed in the United States of America

"Amidst the pixels and algorithms, let us not forget the heartbeat of humanity pulsing beneath the digital surface. In the vast expanse of cyberspace, may our connections be genuine, our laughter infectious, and our humanity ever-present."

CHIMEZIE IGWE

CONTENTS

Copyright
Epigraph
Preface
Chapter 1   1
The Digital Dilemma   2
The Impact of Digital Distraction   3
The Rise of the Digital Detox   4
Finding Balance in the Digital Age   5
Conclusion: Navigating the Digital Maze   6
Chapter 2   7
The Heart of the Matter: Understanding Connection   8
Cracking the Connection Code: Embracing Vulnerability   9
The Power of Presence: Being Here Now   10
Nurturing Connection in the Digital Age: Balancing Screens and Souls   11
Conclusion: Embracing the Magic of Connection   13
Chapter 3   14
The Digital Dilemma: A Tangled Web of Challenges   15
Conquering the Digital Dragons: Strategies for Survival   16
Conclusion: Thriving in the Digital Wilderness   18
Chapter 4   19

The Authenticity Conundrum: Navigating the Sea of Selfies	20
Strategies for Authentic Connection: Cracking the Code	21
Conclusion: Authentically Yours	23
Chapter 5	24
The Digital Communication Revolution: From Smoke Signals to Snapchat	25
Enhancing Connection through Technology: Strategies for Success	26
Conclusion: Connecting in the Digital Age	28
Chapter 6	29
The Empathy Equation: Cracking the Code	30
Strategies for Cultivating Empathy Online: A User's Guide	31
Conclusion: Empathy Unplugged	33
Chapter 7	34
The Lonely Road: Navigating the Digital Desert	35
Cultivating Community in the Digital Desert: Strategies for Success	36
The Importance of Digital Connection	38
Overcoming the Challenges of Digital Connection	39
Conclusion: From Pixels to People	40
Chapter 8	41
The Digital Dilemma: Caught in the Web of Screens	42
Prioritizing Real-Life Interactions: The Art of the Balancing Act	43
Finding Harmony in the Digital Dance	45
Overcoming Digital Distractions: Tips and Tricks	46
Conclusion: The Art of the Screen Time Tango	47
Chapter 9	48
The Rise of the Digital Workplace: Where Pixels Meet	49

Productivity

Fostering Connections in the Digital Workplace: Strategies for Success — 50

Navigating the Challenges of Remote Work Relationships — 52

Conclusion: Building Bridges in the Digital Workplace — 53

Chapter 10 — 54

The Digital Landscape: Where Pixels and Parenthood Collide — 55

Fostering Connection in the Digital Age: Strategies for Success — 56

Navigating the Challenges of Parenting in the Digital Age — 58

Conclusion: Navigating the Digital Jungle — 59

Chapter 11 — 60

The Evolution of Connection: From Smoke Signals to Social Media — 61

Trends Shaping the Future of Connection — 62

Innovations Driving Connection in the Digital Age — 64

The Importance of Human Connection in a Digital World — 66

Navigating the Future of Connection — 67

Conclusion: Embracing the Digital Frontier — 68

Conclusion — 69

The Digital Odyssey: From Dial-Up Dreams to TikTok Triumphs — 70

Navigating the Connection Maze: Tips, Tricks, and LOLs — 71

The Heart of Connection: Pixels, People, and Plenty of LOLs — 73

In Conclusion: Let's LOL our way through the Digital Maze — 74

PREFACE

Navigating the Digital Seas

Welcome, dear reader, to a voyage through the vast and ever-changing landscape of the digital world. As we embark on this journey together, I invite you to set sail with an open mind, a curious spirit, and a hearty sense of humor.

In today's interconnected age, where bytes travel at the speed of light and information flows like a mighty river, navigating the digital seas can be both exhilarating and daunting. From the rise of social media to the dawn of artificial intelligence, the digital revolution has reshaped the way we live, work, and connect with one another in ways that were once unimaginable.

But amidst the dazzling array of gadgets, gizmos, and virtual wonders, it's easy to lose sight of the human element—the laughter, the love, the connections that make life worth living. As we embark on this digital odyssey, let us not forget that behind every pixel, there lies a person—a friend, a family member, a fellow traveler on the journey of life.

So, dear reader, join me as we navigate the digital seas, exploring the trends, innovations, and insights that shape our digital landscape. Together, let us discover the power of connection, the joy of laughter, and the beauty of the human spirit in a world where pixels and people collide.

Fair winds and following seas,

Chimezie Igwe

CHAPTER 1
Welcome to the Digital Jumble: Where Connections Click and Clatter

Hey there, digital adventurers! Ready to embark on a journey through the tangled web of the digital age? Grab your virtual compass and buckle up because we're about to navigate the wild terrain where friendships are made in 280 characters or less, and emojis speak louder than words. Welcome to the land of Instagram stories, Facebook likes, and Twitter retweets—where connection reigns supreme, but authenticity can sometimes feel as rare as a unicorn sighting.

In this chapter, we're diving headfirst into the digital jumble to uncover the impact of our hyper-connected world on the delicate art of relationships. So, hold onto your hats (or should I say, hold onto your smartphones?), because things are about to get enlightening!

THE DIGITAL DILEMMA

Picture this: you're scrolling through your Instagram feed, double-tapping on perfectly curated snapshots of your friends' lives, when suddenly, a notification pops up—a message from an old high school acquaintance you haven't spoken to in years. It's a digital reunion! But as you exchange pleasantries and emojis, you can't help but wonder: does this fleeting interaction truly constitute a meaningful connection?

Welcome to the paradox of the digital age, where we're more connected than ever before, yet often feel lonelier than ever. Our smartphones and social media platforms promise to bring us closer together, but in reality, they can sometimes drive us further apart. The constant barrage of notifications, the pressure to present a polished version of ourselves online, and the superficiality of digital interactions can all erode the depth and authenticity of our relationships.

THE IMPACT OF DIGITAL DISTRACTION

Let's face it: we live in a world of constant distraction. With smartphones buzzing in our pockets and notifications clamoring for our attention, it's no wonder our real-life interactions sometimes take a backseat to our digital dalliances. How many times have you found yourself engrossed in a conversation with a friend, only to be interrupted by the insistent ping of a text message or the allure of a trending Twitter thread?

But here's the kicker: every time we prioritize our screens over the people right in front of us, we chip away at the foundation of our relationships. Eye contact becomes fleeting, conversations become fragmented, and genuine connection becomes a casualty of our digital distractions.

THE RISE OF THE DIGITAL DETOX

So, what's a digital denizen to do in a world overrun by notifications and distractions? Enter the digital detox—a radical act of rebellion against the relentless onslaught of screens and social media. Picture it: a weekend retreat in the wilderness, far from the siren song of Wi-Fi signals and Instagram likes. It's just you, nature, and the blissful absence of digital noise.

But the digital detox isn't just about unplugging—it's about reconnecting. It's about rediscovering the simple joys of face to-face conversation, of laughter shared over a meal, of moments untainted by the glare of a screen. By stepping away from our devices and immersing ourselves in the present moment, we create space for meaningful connections to flourish.

FINDING BALANCE IN THE DIGITAL AGE

Of course, abandoning our digital devices altogether isn't a practical solution for most of us. After all, technology has enriched our lives in countless ways, from keeping us connected with loved ones across the globe to empowering us to pursue our passions and interests.

So, how do we strike a balance between the benefits of technology and the need for genuine human connection? It's all about setting boundaries, practicing mindfulness, and prioritizing quality over quantity in our digital interactions. Whether it's scheduling regular screen-free time with loved ones, establishing tech-free zones in our homes, or simply being more intentional about how we use our devices, there are countless ways we can reclaim control over our digital lives and nurture meaningful relationships in the process.

CONCLUSION: NAVIGATING THE DIGITAL MAZE

And there you have it, fellow digital adventurers—a whirlwind tour through the labyrinth of the digital age, complete with all its pitfalls and possibilities. From the highs of virtual reunions to the lows of digital distractions, we've explored the impact of technology on the delicate dance of relationships.

But fear not, intrepid explorers, for the journey is far from over. In the chapters that follow, we'll delve deeper into the nuances of digital connection, uncovering the secrets to fostering genuine relationships in a world overrun by screens and status updates. So, pack your virtual bags and prepare for the adventure of a lifetime—because in the digital maze of relationships, the only way out is through.

CHAPTER 2
Unraveling the Mysteries of Connection: It's More Than Just Wi-Fi Bars!

Greetings, fellow connection enthusiasts! Today, we embark on an exhilarating expedition into the captivating realm of human connection. So, fasten your seatbelts, grab a cozy blanket, and prepare for an odyssey through the intricate web of social bonds that make life truly meaningful. In this chapter, we're delving deep into the essence of connection, uncovering its profound significance, and unveiling the secrets to fostering authentic relationships. Let's embark on this journey together, shall we?

THE HEART OF THE MATTER: UNDERSTANDING CONNECTION

Connection—it's a word we hear often, but what does it truly mean? At its essence, connection is the invisible force that links us to one another, weaving a rich tapestry of relationships that enrich our lives. It's the feeling of belonging, the shared moments of laughter and tears, and the deep sense of understanding that transcends words. In a world brimming with digital distractions and superficial encounters, authentic connection stands as a beacon of light, guiding us toward deeper fulfillment and genuine intimacy.

Imagine, for a moment, a world devoid of connection—a desolate landscape where hearts remain isolated and souls yearn for companionship. It's a chilling thought, isn't it? Fortunately, the human spirit is inherently drawn to connection, seeking out kindred spirits to share in life's joys and sorrows. From the warmth of a hug to the tender words of affirmation, connection nourishes our spirits and sustains us through life's trials and triumphs.

CRACKING THE CONNECTION CODE: EMBRACING VULNERABILITY

Now, let's talk about the secret ingredient that fuels authentic connection: vulnerability. Picture vulnerability as the key that unlocks the door to deeper intimacy, inviting others into the inner chambers of our hearts. It's the courage to peel back the layers of self-protection and reveal our true selves—the messy, imperfect, beautifully human beings that we are.

But here's the catch: vulnerability can be downright terrifying. It requires us to confront our fears of rejection and judgment, to brave the storm of uncertainty in pursuit of genuine connection. Yet, it is precisely in our moments of vulnerability that we forge the strongest bonds with others. When we dare to show our authentic selves—flaws and all—we create space for others to do the same, fostering an environment of mutual trust and acceptance.

Consider, for instance, a heartfelt conversation with a close friend where you share your deepest fears and dreams. In that moment of vulnerability, you invite your friend into the sacred chambers of your heart, forging a bond that transcends superficial niceties. It's in these raw, unguarded moments that true connection blossoms, enriching both parties in ways that words alone cannot express.

THE POWER OF PRESENCE: BEING HERE NOW

In a world awash with distractions, the art of presence has become a rare and precious commodity. Yet, it is precisely in our moments of presence that connection flourishes most brightly. Picture presence as the gentle current that carries us into the flow of life, anchoring us firmly in the here and now.

When we are truly present with another person—listening with our full attention, engaging with empathy, and responding with authenticity—we create a space for genuine connection to blossom. It's about more than just hearing the words that are spoken; it's about tuning into the unspoken nuances—the subtle shifts in tone, the fleeting expressions—that reveal the true essence of the other person.

Think back to a time when you felt truly seen and heard by another person. Perhaps it was during a heartfelt conversation with a loved one or a shared moment of laughter with a friend. In those moments of deep connection, time seemed to stand still as you basked in the warmth of mutual understanding and acceptance. That, dear reader, is the power of presence in action.

NURTURING CONNECTION IN THE DIGITAL AGE: BALANCING SCREENS AND SOULS

In an era dominated by screens and social media, cultivating authentic connections can feel like navigating a labyrinthine maze. Yet, amidst the digital cacophony, opportunities for genuine connection abound—if only we dare to seize them. It's about striking a delicate balance between our online personas and our real-life relationships, leveraging technology as a tool for connection rather than a barrier to intimacy.

Consider, for instance, the role of social media in modern relationships. While platforms like Facebook and Instagram offer unparalleled opportunities for connection and community, they also present a minefield of comparison and self-doubt. It's all too easy to fall into the trap of measuring our worth by the number of likes and followers we accrue, losing sight of the real connections that lie beneath the surface.

Yet, with mindful intentionality, we can harness the power of social media to deepen our relationships and cultivate genuine connections. It's about using technology as a means to facilitate meaningful interactions rather than replace them, leveraging platforms to share our authentic selves and forge deeper bonds with others.

Consider, for instance, the rise of virtual communities and online support groups, where individuals from around the globe come together to share their stories, offer support, and find solace in shared experiences. In these digital spaces, barriers of geography and circumstance melt away as strangers become friends and allies in the journey of life.

CONCLUSION: EMBRACING THE MAGIC OF CONNECTION

And so, dear reader, we come to the end of our journey through the enchanting realm of human connection. From the depths of vulnerability to the heights of presence, we've explored the intricacies of forging authentic relationships in a digital age. So, the next time you find yourself yearning for deeper connection, remember: vulnerability is your superpower, presence is your secret weapon, and the world is ripe with opportunities for meaningful connection. Embrace the magic of connection, dear reader, and watch as your life is transformed by the power of authentic relationships.

CHAPTER 3
Navigating the Digital Jungle: Challenges and Solutions in the Wild World of Connectivity

Welcome, fellow digital explorers, to the heart of the digital jungle! In this chapter, we're venturing into the dense thicket of challenges that await us in the vast and ever-expanding landscape of the digital realm. But fret not, brave adventurers, for within these challenges lie opportunities for growth, resilience, and triumph. So, strap on your metaphorical boots and grab your virtual compasses, because we're about to embark on an epic quest through the tangled undergrowth of the digital wilderness.

THE DIGITAL DILEMMA: A TANGLED WEB OF CHALLENGES

Ah, the digital age—a marvel of innovation and progress, yet also a labyrinth of complexities and contradictions. As denizens of this digital world, we find ourselves grappling with an array of challenges that can leave even the most seasoned explorer feeling overwhelmed and disoriented.

At the forefront of our digital struggles lies the omnipresent specter of distraction. Picture it: you sit down at your computer, intent on tackling that important project or diving into a creative endeavor, only to find yourself ensnared by the irresistible allure of social media, cat videos, and clickbait articles. Before you know it, hours have slipped by like grains of sand through your digital hourglass, and your once-productive day has vanished into the ether.

But distractions are just one facet of the multifaceted digital dilemma we face. There's also the insidious underbelly of online toxicity—a dark and foreboding realm where trolls lurk in the shadows, ready to unleash their venomous barbs of hate and vitriol upon unsuspecting victims. From cyberbullying to harassment to the spread of misinformation, the digital landscape is rife with dangers that threaten to erode our sense of safety, security, and sanity.

CONQUERING THE DIGITAL DRAGONS: STRATEGIES FOR SURVIVAL

But fear not, fellow adventurers, for every challenge in the digital jungle presents an opportunity for growth and resilience. It's time to sharpen our swords, hone our skills, and prepare to do battle with the digital dragons that threaten to derail our journey. Here are a few strategies to help you navigate the treacherous terrain of the digital realm:

1. **Mindfulness Meditation:** In a world of constant distraction and information overload, mindfulness meditation serves as a beacon of calm amidst the storm. By cultivating mindfulness—the practice of being fully present in the moment—we can learn to anchor ourselves in the here and now, reclaiming our focus and clarity amid the chaos of the digital jungle. So, the next time you feel yourself being swept away by the tidal wave of digital stimuli, take a deep breath, center yourself, and reconnect with the present moment.

2. **Digital Detox:** Sometimes, the best way to conquer the digital dragons is to retreat from the battlefield altogether. That's where the digital detox comes in—a strategic withdrawal from the relentless onslaught of screens and notifications. Whether it's a weekend

retreat in the wilderness, a week-long hiatus from social media, or simply setting aside designated tech-free hours each day, a digital detox can provide much-needed respite from the ceaseless demands of the digital world, allowing us to recharge, refocus, and reconnect with ourselves and those around us.

3. **Setting Boundaries:** In the digital jungle, boundaries are your best defense against the encroaching forces of distraction and toxicity. Whether it's setting limits on your screen time, establishing tech-free zones in your home, or implementing ground rules for digital etiquette in your relationships, setting boundaries empowers you to take control of your digital destiny and reclaim your sense of agency in the digital realm.

4. **Cultivating Digital Literacy:** In an age of misinformation, disinformation, and fake news, digital literacy is more important than ever. By honing your critical thinking skills, sharpening your bullshit detector, and becoming savvy consumers of digital media, you can navigate the treacherous waters of the digital jungle with confidence and discernment. So, the next time you come across a dubious claim, a suspicious article, or a viral meme that seems too good to be true, don't be afraid to dig deeper, question everything, and separate fact from fiction.

CONCLUSION: THRIVING IN THE DIGITAL WILDERNESS

And so, dear adventurers, we emerge from the tangled undergrowth of the digital jungle, weary yet triumphant, having vanquished the digital dragons that once threatened to derail our journey. Armed with mindfulness, resilience, and a healthy dose of digital literacy, we stand ready to navigate the ever-changing landscape of the digital realm with confidence and courage. So, go forth, brave adventurers, and may your journey through the digital wilderness be filled with discovery, growth, and triumph!

CHAPTER 4
Keeping it Real in the Digital Playground: Unveiling the Secrets to Authentic Connections

Hey there, digital trailblazers! Welcome to the land of authenticity in the digital sphere—a place where realness reigns supreme, and authenticity is the name of the game. In this chapter, we're peeling back the layers of digital facades to uncover the true essence of genuine connections. So, grab your virtual magnifying glass and get ready to embark on an enlightening journey through the labyrinth of authenticity in the digital playground.

THE AUTHENTICITY CONUNDRUM: NAVIGATING THE SEA OF SELFIES

Ah, authenticity—the elusive unicorn of the digital age. In a world where filters reign supreme and like to serve as currency, staying true to ourselves can feel like an uphill battle. From meticulously curated Instagram feeds to carefully crafted tweets, the pressure to present a picture-perfect version of ourselves online can sometimes feel suffocating.

But fear not, dear digital denizens, for authenticity is not an endangered species—it's a state of being that resides within every one of us, waiting to be unleashed upon the digital world. It's about embracing our imperfections, celebrating our quirks, and showing up as our true selves, unapologetically and authentically.

STRATEGIES FOR AUTHENTIC CONNECTION: CRACKING THE CODE

So, how do we go about cultivating authentic connections in the digital sphere? It's all about mastering the art of vulnerability, fostering genuine engagement, and embracing the messiness of human connection. Here are a few strategies to help you keep it real in the digital playground:

1. **Embrace Vulnerability:** Authentic connections are forged in the crucible of vulnerability. It's about having the courage to show up as our true selves, flaws and all, and to share our authentic experiences with others. Whether it's opening up about our struggles, sharing our passions, or expressing our true feelings, vulnerability is the key that unlocks the door to deeper connections.

Example: Imagine you're scrolling through your social media feed when you come across a post from a friend who opens up about their recent struggles with anxiety. Instead of scrolling past or offering a generic response, you take a moment to reach out with a heartfelt message of support and solidarity. In that moment of vulnerability, you create a space for authentic connection to flourish.

2. **Cultivate Genuine Engagement:** Authentic connections

thrive on genuine engagement and meaningful interactions. It's about moving beyond surface-level small talk and engaging in conversations that are honest, heartfelt, and authentic. Whether it's sharing stories, asking thoughtful questions, or actively listening to others, genuine engagement is the lifeblood of authentic connections.

Example: Instead of simply liking a friend's post or leaving a generic comment, take the time to engage with their content in a meaningful way. Share your thoughts, ask questions, and spark a conversation that goes beyond the superficial. By engaging authentically with others, you create opportunities for deeper connections to form.

3. **Be Your True Self:** Authenticity begins with embracing who we are and showing up as our true selves, both online and offline. It's about letting go of the need to impress or conform and embracing the unique qualities that make us who we are. Whether it's sharing our passions, expressing our opinions, or owning our quirks, being authentic means being unapologetically ourselves.

Example: Instead of trying to fit into a mold or project a certain image online, be true to yourself and let your personality shine through. Share the things that make you laugh, the causes you're passionate about, and the moments that bring you joy. By being authentically, you, you attract others who resonate with your genuine self.

CONCLUSION: AUTHENTICALLY YOURS

And there you have it, fellow digital adventurers—a roadmap to navigating the digital playground with authenticity and integrity. From embracing vulnerability to cultivating genuine engagement, we've explored the strategies for maintaining authentic connections in the digital sphere. So, the next time you find yourself navigating the digital landscape, remember to stay true to yourself, embrace vulnerability, and keep it real. After all, in a world of filters and facades, authenticity is the greatest gift we can give to ourselves and others.

CHAPTER 5
Dialing Up the Connection: Communication in the Digital Era

Greetings, digital conversationalists! Get ready to dial up your connection game as we delve into the wild world of communication in the digital era. From emojis to GIFs to the art of the perfectly timed meme, we're about to explore how technology can be a powerful tool for enhancing connection and fostering meaningful relationships. So, grab your smartphones and prepare to embark on a journey through the digital landscape of communication!

THE DIGITAL COMMUNICATION REVOLUTION: FROM SMOKE SIGNALS TO SNAPCHAT

Ah, communication—the age-old dance of exchanging ideas, thoughts, and feelings. Throughout history, humans have sought out new ways to connect, from the earliest cave paintings to the invention of the printing press. But never before has communication been so instant, so ubiquitous, and so...emoticon-filled.

Enter the digital era, where communication has undergone a radical transformation, thanks to the wonders of technology. From the humble beginnings of email to the explosion of social media platforms, technology has revolutionized the way we connect, enabling us to communicate across vast distances and disparate time zones with just a few taps of a keyboard.

But with great power comes great responsibility, and the digital age has brought with it a slew of challenges and opportunities when it comes to communication. From navigating the nuances of online interactions to striking a balance between virtual and real-life connections, there's no shortage of topics to explore in the ever-evolving landscape of digital communication.

ENHANCING CONNECTION THROUGH TECHNOLOGY: STRATEGIES FOR SUCCESS

So, how do we harness the power of technology to enhance connection and foster meaningful relationships? It's all about mastering the art of digital communication and leveraging technology as a tool for building bridges, not barriers. Here are a few strategies to help you dial up your connection game in the digital era:

1. **Embrace the Emoji:**

In a world where text-based communication reigns supreme, emojis are the unsung heroes of digital expression. These tiny pictograms have the power to convey emotions, convey nuance, and bridge the gap between words and feelings. So, don't be afraid to sprinkle a few emojis into your digital conversations—they're the secret sauce that adds flavor and personality to your messages.

Example: Instead of simply saying "I'm excited to see you," why not add a couple of exclamation point emojis and a party hat emoji to drive home the excitement? It's like throwing confetti in text form!

2. **Get GIF-y with It:**

GIFs are the cherry on top of the digital communication sundae—fun, expressive, and oh-so-relatable. Whether you're reacting to a funny joke, expressing sympathy, or just adding a touch of whimsy to your messages, GIFs are a versatile tool for enhancing connection and injecting a dose of personality into your digital conversations.

Example: Instead of sending a simple "LOL" in response to a hilarious meme, why not up the ante with a GIF of your favorite comedian doubled over in laughter? It's like bringing the comedy club to your digital doorstep!

3. **Practice Active Listening:**

In the fast-paced world of digital communication, it's easy to get caught up in the frenzy of typing and sending without really stopping to listen. But true connection requires more than just words on a screen—it requires active listening, empathy, and genuine engagement. So, the next time you find yourself in a digital conversation, take a moment to pause, listen, and truly absorb what the other person is saying before crafting your response.

Example: Instead of rushing to type out your next message, take a moment to read and reflect on what the other person has said. Ask follow-up questions, express empathy, and show that you're truly engaged in the conversation. It's like giving the gift of your full attention in a digital world filled with distractions!

CONCLUSION: CONNECTING IN THE DIGITAL AGE

And there you have it, digital communicators—a crash course in enhancing connection through technology. From emojis to GIFs to the art of active listening, we've explored the strategies for building meaningful relationships in the digital era. So, the next time you find yourself navigating the digital landscape of communication, remember to embrace the tools at your disposal, inject a dose of personality into your messages, and above all, strive to foster genuine connections with those around you. After all, in a world of screens and pixels, it's the human connection that truly matters most.

CHAPTER 6
Empathy Unplugged: Nurturing Understanding in the Digital World

Hey there, digital citizens! Get ready to plug into the power of empathy as we journey through the vast and sometimes bewildering landscape of online interactions. In this chapter, we'll uncover the secrets to cultivating empathy and understanding in the digital realm, all while keeping the mood light and the insights flowing. So, grab your virtual magnifying glass and let's dive deep into the heart of empathy in the digital age!

THE EMPATHY EQUATION: CRACKING THE CODE

Empathy—it's the secret sauce that makes the world go around, both online and off. But in a world where screens often act as barriers between us and the people on the other side, nurturing empathy can sometimes feel like an uphill battle. That's where we come in, intrepid explorers of the digital frontier, armed with curiosity, compassion, and maybe just a touch of humor.

At its core, empathy is about putting ourselves in someone else's shoes, seeing the world through their eyes, and understanding their thoughts, feelings, and experiences. It's like a superpower that allows us to forge deeper connections, bridge divides, and foster a sense of understanding and compassion in our online interactions.

STRATEGIES FOR CULTIVATING EMPATHY ONLINE: A USER'S GUIDE

So, how do we go about cultivating empathy in the digital realm? It's all about embracing curiosity, practicing active listening, and making space for diverse perspectives to thrive. Here are a few strategies to help you tap into the power of empathy online:

1. **Walk a Mile in Their Digital Shoes:**

Empathy begins with curiosity—the willingness to step outside of our own experiences and see the world through someone else's eyes. So, the next time you encounter a perspective that differs from your own online, resist the urge to dismiss or debate, and instead, approach it with an open mind and a genuine desire to understand.

Example: Imagine you come across a social media post expressing a viewpoint that clashes with your own. Instead of immediately jumping into the fray with arguments and counterarguments, take a moment to pause and consider the perspective of the person behind the screen. What experiences or beliefs might have led them to hold this viewpoint? By approaching the conversation with curiosity rather than defensiveness, you create space for empathy to flourish.

2. **Practice Active Listening:**

In the fast-paced world of digital communication, it's easy to get caught up in the frenzy of typing and sending without really stopping to listen. But true empathy requires more than just words on a screen—it requires active listening, genuine engagement, and a willingness to truly hear what the other person is saying.

Example: Next time you find yourself engaged in a digital conversation, whether it's a heated debate or a casual exchange, make a conscious effort to practice active listening. Instead of formulating your response while the other person is speaking, take a moment to truly absorb their words, ask clarifying questions, and show that you're genuinely engaged in the conversation. By practicing active listening, you create space for empathy to thrive and understanding to blossom.

3. **Create Space for Diverse Perspectives:**

Empathy thrives in environments where diverse perspectives are valued, respected, and celebrated. So, whether you're moderating an online community, participating in a group chat, or simply scrolling through your social media feed, make an effort to create space for voices that might otherwise go unheard.

Example: Consider joining online forums or groups that are dedicated to fostering empathy, understanding, and dialogue across diverse perspectives. Engage with people from different backgrounds, cultures, and experiences, and be open to learning from their unique viewpoints. By actively seeking out diverse perspectives and making space for them to be heard, you contribute to a more empathetic and inclusive digital community.

CONCLUSION: EMPATHY UNPLUGGED

And there you have it, digital adventurers—a crash course in cultivating empathy and understanding in the digital realm. From embracing curiosity to practicing active listening to creating space for diverse perspectives, we've explored the strategies for nurturing empathy online. So, the next time you find yourself navigating the digital landscape, remember to approach each interaction with an open mind, a compassionate heart, and a willingness to truly understand the perspectives of others. After all, in a world where screens often act as barriers, empathy is the bridge that connects us all.

CHAPTER 7
From Lonely to Connected: Building Community in the Digital Realm

Hey there, digital wanderers! Ever feel like you're navigating the vast expanse of the internet all alone? Fear not, because, in this chapter, we're diving headfirst into the deep end of overcoming loneliness and finding your tribe in the bustling metropolis of the digital world. So, grab your virtual handkerchiefs and get ready for a rollercoaster ride through the highs and lows of digital connection!

THE LONELY ROAD: NAVIGATING THE DIGITAL DESERT

Loneliness—it's the invisible shadow that lurks in the corners of our screens, waiting to pounce when we least expect it. In a world where likes and followers can sometimes feel like poor substitutes for real human connection, it's easy to find yourself adrift in a sea of pixels, longing for the warmth of genuine companionship.

But fear not, fellow digital nomads, for the digital landscape is teeming with oases of connection just waiting to be discovered. From online communities to virtual hangouts to social media groups, there are countless opportunities to forge meaningful connections and build lasting relationships in the digital realm.

CULTIVATING COMMUNITY IN THE DIGITAL DESERT: STRATEGIES FOR SUCCESS

So, how do we go about overcoming loneliness and finding community in the digital wilderness? It's all about stepping out of your comfort zone, embracing vulnerability, and seeking out spaces where you can be your authentic self. Here are a few strategies to help you navigate the digital desert and find your tribe:

1. **Join Online Communities:**

Online communities are like bustling town squares in the digital landscape—vibrant, diverse, and full of opportunities for connection. Whether you're passionate about a particular hobby, interest, or cause, there's bound to be an online community out there where you can find like-minded individuals to connect with.

Example: Imagine you're a budding plant parent looking to connect with other green-thumbed enthusiasts. Joining an online gardening community could provide the perfect opportunity to share tips, swap stories, and forge friendships with fellow plant lovers from around the world. Who knew gardening could be so social?

2. Attend Virtual Events:

In the age of social distancing, virtual events have become the digital equivalent of neighborhood block parties—a chance to come together, share experiences, and build connections from the comfort of your own home. Whether it's a virtual concert, a live-streamed workshop, or a digital book club, attending virtual events can be a great way to meet new people and expand your social circle.

Example: Picture yourself tuning in to a virtual cooking class hosted by a celebrity chef. As you follow along with the recipe and chat with other participants in the virtual chatroom, you find yourself connecting with fellow foodies over your shared love of culinary adventures. Who knows, you might even find a new cooking buddy to swap recipes with!

3. Reach Out and Connect:

In the digital world, connection is just a click away. So, don't be afraid to reach out and connect with people who catch your eye or spark your interest online. Whether it's sending a friendly message, leaving a comment on a post, or joining a conversation in a group chat, reaching out is the first step toward building meaningful connections in the digital realm.

Example: Imagine you come across a social media post from someone who shares your love of vintage vinyl records. Instead of just scrolling past, why not shoot them a message introducing yourself and sharing a few of your favorite albums? Before you know it, you could be swapping music recommendations and bonding over your shared passion for analog sound.

THE IMPORTANCE OF DIGITAL CONNECTION

In an increasingly digital world, the importance of cultivating meaningful connections online cannot be overstated. While it's easy to dismiss digital interactions as shallow or superficial, the reality is that the bonds we forge in the digital realm can be just as deep and meaningful as those formed in face-to-face interactions.

Digital connections have the power to transcend geographical boundaries, cultural differences, and even language barriers, allowing us to connect with people from all walks of life and build bridges across divides. Whether it's finding support in an online community, sharing moments of joy and laughter in a virtual hangout, or forging lifelong friendships through social media, the connections we make online have the potential to enrich our lives in ways we never thought possible.

OVERCOMING THE CHALLENGES OF DIGITAL CONNECTION

Of course, building meaningful connections in the digital realm isn't always easy. From navigating the pitfalls of online anonymity to dealing with trolls and cyberbullies, there are plenty of challenges that can stand in the way of forming genuine connections online. But by approaching digital connection with intentionality, authenticity, and a healthy dose of resilience, we can overcome these challenges and create spaces where empathy, understanding, and community can thrive.

CONCLUSION: FROM PIXELS TO PEOPLE

And there you have it, digital adventurers—a roadmap to overcoming loneliness and finding community in the digital wilderness. From joining online communities to attending virtual events to reaching out and connecting with others, we've explored the strategies for building meaningful relationships in the digital realm. So, the next time you find yourself feeling lonely in the digital desert, remember that you're not alone—there's a whole world of digital companionship waiting to be discovered, one clicks at a time.

CHAPTER 8
Screen Time Tango: Striking the Right Balance Between Pixels and People

Hey there, screen time aficionados! Ready to embark on a journey through the digital dance floor as we master the art of balancing our online and offline worlds? In this chapter, we'll unravel the secrets to prioritizing real-life interactions while still savoring the sweet symphony of the digital realm. So, kick off your virtual shoes, and let's dive into the Screen Time Tango!

THE DIGITAL DILEMMA: CAUGHT IN THE WEB OF SCREENS

Ah, screen time—the double-edged sword of the digital age. With smartphones in our pockets, laptops on our laps, and tablets at our fingertips, it's all too easy to get sucked into the vortex of endless scrolling and mindless tapping. Before we know it, hours have passed, and we find ourselves lost in the digital labyrinth, disconnected from the world around us.

But fear not, intrepid adventurers, for finding balance in the digital dance isn't just possible—it's essential for our well-being. By prioritizing real-life interactions and carving out space for offline connections, we can reclaim our time, nurture meaningful relationships, and live our lives to the fullest, both online and off.

PRIORITIZING REAL-LIFE INTERACTIONS: THE ART OF THE BALANCING ACT

So, how do we go about prioritizing real-life interactions in a world dominated by screens? It's all about embracing intentionality, setting boundaries, and being mindful of how we allocate our time and attention. Here are a few strategies to help you strike the right balance between pixels and people:

1. **Set Boundaries with Technology:**

Technology is a powerful tool, but like any tool, it's important to use it mindfully and in moderation. Set boundaries around your screen time by establishing designated "tech-free" zones and times during the day when you commit to putting away your devices and engaging fully with the world around you.

Example: Designate your bedroom as a tech-free zone and banish smartphones, tablets, and laptops from your sleeping sanctuary. Instead of scrolling through social media before bed, opt for a relaxing bedtime routine that promotes restful sleep, such as reading a book, practicing mindfulness, or journaling.

2. **Schedule Regular Screen-Free Activities:**

Incorporate regular screen-free activities into your daily routine to balance out the time spent in front of screens. Whether it's going for a walk-in nature, meeting up with friends for a coffee date, or pursuing a hobby you're passionate about, make time for activities that nourish your soul and foster real-life connections.

Example: Dedicate one evening a week to hosting a screen-free game night with friends or family. Break out the board games, card games, or puzzles and spend quality time together laughing, bonding, and creating memories without the distractions of screens.

3. **Practice Presence in Real-Life Interactions:**

When you're spending time with loved ones in real life, be fully present and engaged in the moment. Put away your devices, resist the urge to check your notifications, and give the people you're with your undivided attention. By prioritizing quality over quantity in your real-life interactions, you'll strengthen your relationships and create meaningful memories that last a lifetime.

Example: Imagine you're out for dinner with friends at your favorite restaurant. Instead of keeping your phone on the table and periodically checking for updates, tuck it away in your bag or pocket and focus on enjoying the conversation, savoring the food, and connecting with the people around you.

FINDING HARMONY IN THE DIGITAL DANCE

In a world where screens often act as barriers to genuine connection, finding harmony in digital dance requires intentionality, mindfulness, and a commitment to prioritizing real-life interactions. By setting boundaries with technology, scheduling regular screen-free activities, and practicing presence in real-life interactions, we can strike the right balance between pixels and people and live our lives with purpose, connection, and joy.

OVERCOMING DIGITAL DISTRACTIONS: TIPS AND TRICKS

Of course, balancing screen time and prioritizing real-life interactions isn't always easy. From the siren call of social media to the constant barrage of notifications, there are plenty of digital distractions that can derail our best-laid plans for offline connection. But fear not, dear readers, for there are plenty of tips and tricks to help you overcome digital distractions and stay focused on what truly matters.

CONCLUSION: THE ART OF THE SCREEN TIME TANGO

And there you have it, digital dancers—a crash course in striking the right balance between pixels and people. From setting boundaries with technology to scheduling regular screen-free activities to practicing presence in real-life interactions, we've explored the strategies for prioritizing real-life interactions in the digital age. So, the next time you find yourself caught in the digital dance, remember to step back, take a deep breath, and prioritize the connections that nourish your soul and bring you joy, both online and off.

CHAPTER 9
From Cubicle Comrades to Virtual Vibe-Mates: Nurturing Relationships in the Digital Workplace

Hey there, digital work warriors! Ready to dive into the virtual realm and master the art of nurturing relationships in the ever-evolving landscape of the digital workplace? In this chapter, we'll unpack the secrets to fostering meaningful connections, building camaraderie, and cultivating a sense of community—even when we're miles apart. So, grab your virtual coffee mugs, and let's embark on a journey through the digital corridors of the modern workplace!

THE RISE OF THE DIGITAL WORKPLACE: WHERE PIXELS MEET PRODUCTIVITY

Ah, the digital workplace—a brave new world where cubicles have been replaced by Zoom squares, watercooler chats have migrated to Slack channels, and the office commute consists of shuffling from the bedroom to the living room. In this digital age of remote work and virtual collaboration, nurturing relationships in the workplace has taken on a whole new meaning.

But fear not, intrepid telecommuters, for the digital workplace is ripe with opportunities for connection and camaraderie. From virtual team-building activities to online coffee chats to collaborative project management tools, there are countless ways to foster meaningful relationships and build a sense of community in the digital realm.

FOSTERING CONNECTIONS IN THE DIGITAL WORKPLACE: STRATEGIES FOR SUCCESS

So, how do we go about nurturing relationships in the digital workplace and fostering a sense of belonging among remote teams? It's all about embracing creativity, communication, and a healthy dose of humor. Here are a few strategies to help you navigate the digital corridors of the modern workplace:

1. **Embrace Virtual Team-Building Activities:**

Just because your miles apart don't mean you can't have a little fun together! Embrace virtual team-building activities as a way to foster connections and build camaraderie among remote teams. Whether it's a virtual happy hour, an online game night, or a virtual escape room challenge, there are plenty of ways to bring your team together and strengthen bonds in the digital realm.

Example: Imagine organizing a virtual trivia night for your team, complete with themed rounds, funny trivia questions, and virtual prizes. As your teammates compete to see who knows the most obscure facts, you'll have the opportunity to bond over shared laughter, friendly competition, and a sense of camaraderie that transcends physical distance.

2. **Cultivate Open Communication Channels:**

Communication is the lifeblood of any successful relationship, and the digital workplace is no exception. Cultivate open communication channels among remote teams, whether it's through video meetings, instant messaging platforms, or collaborative project management tools. Encourage team members to share ideas, ask questions, and express themselves freely, creating a culture of openness and transparency that fosters trust and collaboration.

Example: Consider creating a dedicated Slack channel or Microsoft Teams group for casual conversations and water cooler chats. Encourage team members to share funny memes, interesting articles, or updates about their lives outside of work, creating opportunities for connection and camaraderie beyond the confines of formal meetings and project discussions.

3. **Celebrate Milestones and Achievements:**

In the fast-paced world of remote work, it's easy to overlook the little victories and milestones that make each day special. Take the time to celebrate achievements and milestones, whether it's hitting a project deadline, reaching a sales target, or simply making it through another busy week. By acknowledging and celebrating the accomplishments of your team members, you'll not only boost morale and motivation but also strengthen bonds and foster a sense of belonging in the digital workplace.

Example: Imagine organizing a virtual "Friday Funday" to celebrate the end of the week and recognize the hard work and dedication of your team. Host a virtual awards ceremony to recognize standout performances, share success stories and shoutouts, and toast to another week of teamwork and collaboration. It's like throwing a virtual party to celebrate the achievements of your digital dream team!

NAVIGATING THE CHALLENGES OF REMOTE WORK RELATIONSHIPS

Of course, nurturing relationships in the digital workplace isn't without its challenges. From navigating time zone differences to overcoming communication barriers, there are plenty of obstacles that can stand in the way of building meaningful connections and fostering a sense of community among remote teams. But by approaching these challenges with creativity, empathy, and a spirit of collaboration, we can overcome them and create thriving virtual work environments where every team member feels valued, supported, and connected.

CONCLUSION: BUILDING BRIDGES IN THE DIGITAL WORKPLACE

And there you have it, digital work warriors—a roadmap to nurturing relationships in the digital workplace and fostering a sense of community among remote teams. From embracing virtual team-building activities to cultivating open communication channels to celebrating milestones and achievements, we've explored the strategies for building bridges in the digital workplace. So, the next time you find yourself navigating the digital corridors of the modern workplace, remember to embrace creativity, communication, and connection as you journey together with your virtual vibe-mates toward success and fulfillment in the digital realm.

CHAPTER 10
Raising Digital Natives: How to Stay Connected with Your Tech-Savvy Tykes

Hey there, fellow digital trailblazers! Are you ready to embark on a wild ride through the digital jungle as we navigate the ins and outs of parenting in the age of smartphones, tablets, and TikTok? In this chapter, we'll uncover the secrets to fostering connection with your tech-savvy tots, all while keeping the mood light and the insights flowing. So, buckle up and get ready for a journey through the digital wilderness of modern parenting!

THE DIGITAL LANDSCAPE: WHERE PIXELS AND PARENTHOOD COLLIDE

Ah, the digital age—a brave new world where toddlers can swipe before they can walk and bedtime stories come in the form of interactive apps. As parents, navigating the ever-changing landscape of technology can feel like embarking on a jungle safari, with new challenges and adventures lurking around every corner.

But fear not, fellow adventurers, for connecting with your digital natives is not only possible but also essential for their growth and development. From setting boundaries around screen time to fostering open communication about online safety, there are plenty of strategies to help you stay connected with your tech-savvy tykes and raise healthy, happy digital citizens.

FOSTERING CONNECTION IN THE DIGITAL AGE: STRATEGIES FOR SUCCESS

So, how do we go about fostering connection with our children in the digital age? It's all about finding balance, setting boundaries, and leading by example. Here are a few strategies to help you navigate the digital landscape of modern parenting:

1. **Lead by Example:**

As the saying goes, children learn more from what you do than what you say. So, lead by example when it comes to your technology use. Show your children that technology is a tool to be used mindfully and responsibly by modeling healthy screen habits and setting boundaries around your device use.

Example: Instead of constantly checking your phone during family meals or outings, make a conscious effort to put it away and be fully present with your children. By showing them that you prioritize quality time together over digital distractions, you'll set a positive example for healthy screen habits and foster a deeper connection with your kids.

2. **Create Tech-Free Zones and Times:**

In a world where screens can easily take over our lives, it's important to carve out tech-free zones and times where devices are off-limits. Designate certain areas of your home, such as the dinner table or bedrooms, as tech-free zones, and establish regular tech-free times, such as during family meals or before bedtime, to promote face-to-face interaction and quality time together.

Example: Consider implementing a "digital detox" hour each evening where the whole family unplugs from screens and engages in tech-free activities together, such as playing board games, reading books, or going for a walk. By creating space for unplugged connections, you'll strengthen your bond with your children and create lasting memories that go beyond the digital realm.

3. **Have Open and Honest Conversations:**

Communication is key when it comes to fostering connection with your children in the digital age. Have open and honest conversations with them about technology, online safety, and responsible digital citizenship. Encourage them to ask questions, share their experiences, and express their concerns, creating a safe and supportive environment where they feel comfortable talking to you about their digital lives.

Example: Sit down with your children and have a family meeting to discuss your family's digital rules and expectations. Talk to them about the importance of balancing screen time with other activities, such as homework, hobbies, and outdoor play, and empower them to make responsible choices when it comes to their device use. By involving them in the conversation and giving them a voice in setting family rules, you'll foster a sense of ownership and accountability when it comes to technology use.

NAVIGATING THE CHALLENGES OF PARENTING IN THE DIGITAL AGE

Of course, parenting in the digital age isn't without its challenges. From navigating the ever-changing landscape of social media to dealing with cyberbullying and online predators, there are plenty of obstacles that can stand in the way of fostering connection with your children in the digital realm. But by staying informed, staying involved, and staying connected, you can overcome these challenges and create a safe and supportive digital environment where your children can thrive.

CONCLUSION: NAVIGATING THE DIGITAL JUNGLE

And there you have it, fellow digital adventurers—a guide to fostering connection with your tech-savvy tykes in the digital age. From leading by example to creating tech-free zones and times to having open and honest conversations, we've explored the strategies for navigating the digital jungle of modern parenting. So, the next time you find yourself embarking on a digital safari with your children, remember to stay connected, stay informed, and stay involved as you journey together through the wild and wonderful world of technology.

CHAPTER 11
The Connection Conundrum: Navigating Trends and Innovations with a Smile

Hey there, fellow connection connoisseurs! Are you ready to embark on a journey into the wild and wacky world of the future of connection? In this chapter, we'll explore the latest trends and innovations shaping the way we connect in the digital age—all while keeping the mood light and the insights flowing. So, grab your virtual magnifying glass, and let's dive into the fascinating frontier of connectivity!

THE EVOLUTION OF CONNECTION: FROM SMOKE SIGNALS TO SOCIAL MEDIA

Ah, connection—it's the lifeblood of human existence, the glue that binds us together across time and space. From ancient cave paintings to carrier pigeons to the advent of the telephone, humanity has always found ingenious ways to connect, transcending barriers of distance and time.

But in the digital age, the landscape of connection is evolving at breakneck speed, with new technologies and innovations reshaping the way we interact and communicate with each other. From social media platforms to virtual reality to artificial intelligence, the future of connection is a brave new world filled with endless possibilities and exciting opportunities.

TRENDS SHAPING THE FUTURE OF CONNECTION

So, what does the future hold for the world of connection? Let's take a closer look at some of the trends and innovations that are shaping the way we connect in the digital age:

1. **The Rise of Virtual Reality (VR):**

Get ready to strap on your VR goggles and step into a whole new dimension of connection! Virtual reality technology is revolutionizing the way we interact and communicate with each other, allowing us to immerse ourselves in digital worlds and connect with others in ways that were once unimaginable.

Example: Imagine attending a virtual concert in the comfort of your own home, where you can dance, chat, and interact with other fans from around the world—all without leaving your living room. With VR technology, the possibilities for connection are limited only by our imagination.

2. **The Era of Augmented Reality (AR):**

Augmented reality is blurring the lines between the digital and physical worlds, allowing us to overlay digital information and experiences onto our real-world surroundings. From interactive shopping experiences to location-based games, AR technology is opening up new avenues for connection and engagement in our everyday lives.

Example: Picture yourself exploring a city with your smartphone in hand, using AR technology to uncover hidden landmarks, discover local history, and connect with other users who share your interests. With AR, the world becomes a playground for connection and discovery, where every street corner holds the potential for a new adventure.

3. The Power of Artificial Intelligence (AI):

Artificial intelligence is revolutionizing the way we connect online, from personalized recommendations on social media platforms to chatbots that provide instant customer support. With AI technology, our digital interactions are becoming more intelligent, intuitive, and tailored to our individual preferences and needs.

Example: Imagine chatting with a virtual assistant powered by AI technology, which can anticipate your needs, answer your questions, and provide personalized recommendations based on your interests and preferences. Whether you're planning a trip, shopping for groceries, or catching up with friends, AI technology is there to help you navigate the digital landscape with ease.

INNOVATIONS DRIVING CONNECTION IN THE DIGITAL AGE

In addition to these emerging trends, there are countless innovations driving connection in the digital age, from social media platforms to messaging apps to collaborative tools. Let's explore some of the most groundbreaking innovations that are shaping the future of connection:

1. **Social Media Platforms:**

Love it or hate it, social media has become an integral part of how we connect with each other in the digital age. From Facebook to Instagram to TikTok, social media platforms are constantly evolving to meet the changing needs and preferences of users, offering new features, functionalities, and ways to connect with friends, family, and followers.

Example: Consider the rise of live streaming on social media platforms, which allows users to broadcast live video content to their followers in real-time. Whether it's sharing a behind-the-scenes look at your day-to-day life or hosting a Q&A session with your audience, live streaming has become a powerful tool for fostering connection and engagement on social media.

2. **Messaging Apps:**

In a world where instant communication is the norm, messaging apps have become indispensable tools for staying connected with friends, family, and colleagues. From WhatsApp to Slack to

WeChat, messaging apps offer a convenient and efficient way to send messages, make voice and video calls, and share media with others, regardless of where they are in the world.

Example: Consider the rise of disappearing messages on messaging apps like Snapchat and Instagram, which allow users to send temporary messages that disappear after a set period. Whether it's sharing a silly selfie or sending a quick update to a friend, disappearing messages offer a fun and ephemeral way to connect with others in the digital realm.

3. **Collaborative Tools:**

With remote work on the rise, collaborative tools have become essential for staying connected and productive in the digital workplace. From project management platforms to video conferencing software to virtual whiteboards, collaborative tools offer a wide range of functionalities designed to streamline communication, facilitate teamwork, and foster connection among remote teams.

Example: Consider the rise of virtual whiteboards, which allow users to brainstorm ideas, organize thoughts, and collaborate on projects in real time, regardless of geographical location. Whether it's mapping out a project timeline, sketching out design ideas, or brainstorming solutions to a problem, virtual whiteboards offer a dynamic and interactive space for teams to come together, share ideas, and work towards common goals.

THE IMPORTANCE OF HUMAN CONNECTION IN A DIGITAL WORLD

Amidst all the technological innovations and digital advancements, it's important to remember the timeless importance of human connection. While technology can facilitate communication and bridge geographical divides, it's the human connections—the bonds of friendship, family, and community—that truly enrich our lives and bring meaning to our digital interactions.

In a world where screens often act as barriers to genuine connection, it's essential to cultivate empathy, understanding, and authenticity in our digital interactions. Whether it's reaching out to a friend in need, sharing a moment of laughter with a loved one, or connecting with like-minded individuals online, the connections we make with others have the power to uplift, inspire, and enrich our lives in ways that technology alone cannot.

NAVIGATING THE FUTURE OF CONNECTION

As we journey into the future of connection, it's important to approach technological innovations with curiosity, adaptability, and a healthy dose of skepticism. While new technologies and trends may offer exciting opportunities for connection and engagement, they also come with their own set of challenges and considerations.

From navigating privacy concerns and online safety to managing screen time and digital overload, it's essential to approach the future of connection with intentionality, mindfulness, and a commitment to fostering meaningful relationships both online and off. By staying informed, staying connected, and staying true to ourselves, we can navigate the ever-changing landscape of connectivity with confidence, curiosity, and compassion.

CONCLUSION: EMBRACING THE DIGITAL FRONTIER

And there you have it, fellow digital pioneers—a glimpse into the future of connection and the trends and innovations shaping the way we connect in the digital age. From virtual reality to augmented reality to artificial intelligence, the future of connection is a wild and wonderful frontier filled with endless possibilities and exciting opportunities.

As we navigate this brave new world of connectivity, let's remember to stay curious, stay connected, and stay true to the values that make us human. Whether it's reaching out to a friend in need, sharing a moment of laughter with a loved one, or connecting with like-minded individuals online, let's embrace the digital frontier with open hearts and open minds, forging connections that enrich our lives and bring us closer together, one pixel at a time.

CONCLUSION
Embracing the Connection Evolution: From Pixels to People, One LOL at a Time

Well, fellow digital adventurers, we've reached the end of our journey through the ever-evolving landscape of connection in the digital age. But before we bid adieu and sign off into the digital sunset, let's take a moment to reflect on the wild ride we've been on and the insights we've uncovered along the way.

THE DIGITAL ODYSSEY: FROM DIAL-UP DREAMS TO TIKTOK TRIUMPHS

Ah, connection—it's the thread that weaves through the fabric of our lives, binding us together across time and space in a tapestry of pixels and people. From the humble beginnings of dial-up internet to the dazzling heights of social media, the digital age has transformed the way we connect, communicate, and relate to one another in ways that were once unimaginable.

But amidst the whirlwind of tweets, likes, and viral videos, it's easy to lose sight of the true essence of connection—the human touch, the warmth of a smile, the laughter shared between friends. As we journey through the digital wilderness, let's remember to keep our hearts open, our minds curious, and our laughter infectious, for its these moments of genuine connection that truly enrich our lives and bring joy to our digital interactions.

NAVIGATING THE CONNECTION MAZE: TIPS, TRICKS, AND LOLS

So, how do we navigate the maze of connection in an ever-evolving world? Fear not, dear readers, for I come bearing insights, solutions, and a healthy dose of humor to guide you on your digital odyssey:

1. **Stay Curious, Stay Connected:**

In a world where technology is constantly evolving, it's important to stay curious and stay connected with the latest trends and innovations shaping the way we connect with each other. Whether it's diving into the world of virtual reality, exploring the possibilities of augmented reality, or embracing the power of artificial intelligence, let your curiosity be your compass as you navigate the digital frontier.

Example: Imagine attending a virtual reality concert with your friends, where you can dance, sing, and interact with your favorite artists in a digital wonderland. With virtual reality technology, the possibilities for connection are limited only by our imagination—so why not dive in and see where the digital rabbit hole takes you?

2. **Balance is Key:**

In our quest for connection, it's important to strike a balance between our digital lives and our real-world interactions. While technology has the power to bring us closer together, it can also drive us apart if we're not careful. So, remember to unplug, unwind, and prioritize face-to-face connections with the people who matter most in your life.

Example: Picture yourself gathering with friends for a cozy game night, complete with board games, snacks, and plenty of laughter. As you roll the dice, draw cards, and compete for victory, you'll forge bonds that go beyond the confines of the digital realm, creating memories that last a lifetime.

3. **Embrace Authenticity:**

In a world where filters and facades often reign supreme, authenticity is the key to true connection. So, embrace your quirks, your flaws, and your imperfections, and let your true self shine through in all your digital interactions. After all, it's your unique personality and perspective that make you truly lovable—and truly unforgettable.

Example: Imagine sharing a funny blooper reel with your friends, showcasing all the silly mistakes and mishaps that make you who you are. By embracing your authentic self and letting your true colors shine, you'll attract genuine connections and create moments of laughter and joy that resonate long after the screen fades to black.

THE HEART OF CONNECTION: PIXELS, PEOPLE, AND PLENTY OF LOLS

As we journey through the digital landscape of connection, let's remember that at the heart of it all, it's the moments of laughter, love, and genuine human connection that truly matter. Whether it's sharing a funny meme with a friend, chatting with loved ones on video calls, or simply enjoying a quiet moment of solitude in the digital wilderness, let's cherish each moment and savor the connections that bring joy to our lives.

So, as you venture forth into the digital unknown, may your hearts be open, your minds curious, and your laughter infectious. And remember, dear readers, that in a world filled with pixels and people, the greatest connection of all is the one we share.

IN CONCLUSION: LET'S LOL OUR WAY THROUGH THE DIGITAL MAZE

And there you have it, fellow digital explorers—a journey through the wild and wacky world of connection in the digital age, complete with laughter, insights, and plenty of LOLs along the way. As we bid adieu to our digital odyssey and set sail into the sunset of cyberspace, let's carry with us the lessons learned, the connections made, and the memories shared, knowing that the greatest adventure of all is the one we embark on together, one LOL at a time.

www.ingramcontent.com/pod-product-compliance
Lightning Source LLC
Chambersburg PA
CBHW070354230526
45471CB00006B/2563